TIM BATTY

press™

New York

Published in 2023 by The Rosen Publishing Group, Inc.
29 East 21st Street, New York, NY 10010

Originally Published in English by Haynes Publishing under the title: *Dinosaurs Pocket Manual* © Haynes Publishing 2019

Cataloging-in-Publication Data

Names: Batty, Tim.
Title: Dinosaurs with plates, horns, and frills / Tim Batty.
Description: New York : PowerKids Press, 2023. | Series: Dinosaur discovery | Includes glossary and index.
Identifiers: ISBN 9781725338418 (pbk.) | ISBN 9781725338432 (library bound) | ISBN 9781725338425 (6 pack) | ISBN 9781725338449 (ebook)
Subjects: LCSH: Dinosaurs--Juvenile literature.
Classification: LCC QE861.5 B38 2023 | DDC 567.9--dc23

Design: Richard Parsons and James Robertson

Picture credits:
Cover: DM7, HitToon, kzww, John Archer, Nenov Brothers Images
De Agostini/NHMPL: 3, 4-5, 6-7, 16-17, 18-19, 28-29
Gareth Monger: 14-15, 20-21
Natural History Museum Picture Library (NHMPL): 3
NOPPHARAT7824: 30-32
John Archer: 2-3
John Sibbick: 8-9
Chris Srnka: 3, 10-11, 12-13, 22-23, 24-25, 26-27

Manufactured in the United States of America

CPSIA Compliance Information: Batch #CSPK23. For further information contact Rosen Publishing, New York, New York at 1-800-237-9932.

Find us on

The Author

Tim Batty was educated at the University of Wolverhampton before entering on a career in museums. He is a "founding father" and curator of The Dinosaur Museum in Dorchester, UK, and his favorite dinosaur is Iguanodon – its fascinating story and past first sparked and inspired his fascination with dinosaurs.

Contents

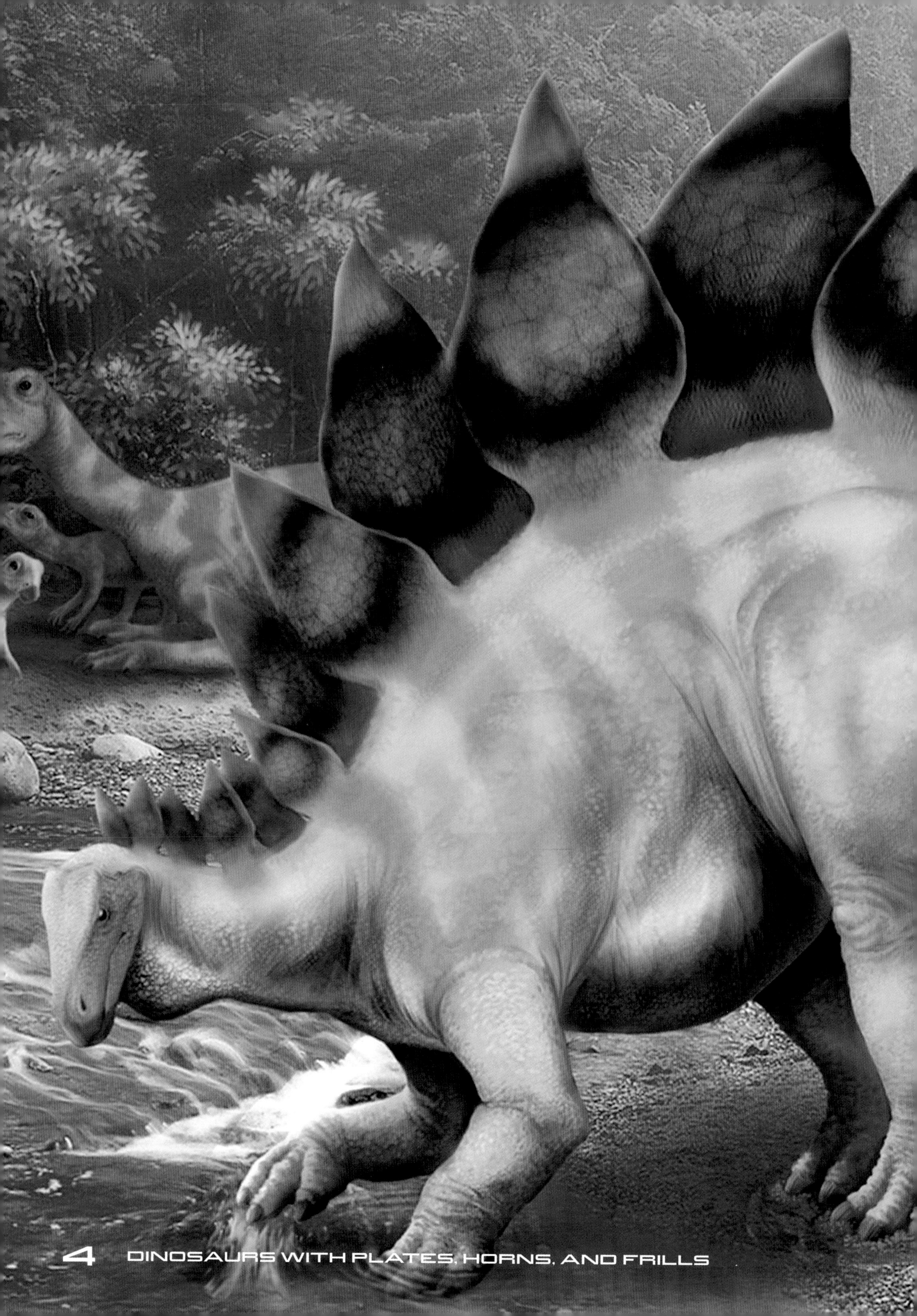

About This Book

This exciting book is packed with all things dino-related, including stunning pictures, fascinating facts, and all the vital statistics. It features 11 species of dinosaurs, from favorites such as *Stegosaurus* and *Triceratops* to the unusual *Therizinosaurus*!

Amargasaurus

Pronounced: *ah-mahr-guh-SAW-ruhs*

The distinctive feature of *Amargasaurus* was a double row of spines attached to its neck, back, and probably tail. The spines were tall, at about 20 inches (50 cm) high, and more angled on the short neck, becoming shorter on the back and tail. The spines were extensions of the vertebrae in the backbone and they were sharp to deter predators. They would have been covered in a hard matter called keratin to give extra strength, similar to the horns of some mammals today. Another purpose of the spines may have been for display. It is thought that *Amargasaurus* was a medium-sized sauropod, similar in many ways to *Diplodocus*. Like all sauropods, *Amargasaurus* had peg-like teeth for raking leaves off branches. However, it could not chew so it needed to swallow gastroliths to help break up food in the stomach. These stones were rough when first swallowed but gradually got worn smooth. *Amargasaurus* shared its habitat with other sauropods but they would have each eaten different food sources to limit competition.

Statistics

Meaning	Amarga Lizard
When	Early Cretaceous
Time	132–127 million years ago
Max length	33 feet (10 m)
Max height	13 feet (4 m)
Max weight	22,000 pounds (10,000 kg)
Stance	Quadruped
Where	Argentina
Diet	Herbivore
Activity	Grazing
Intelligence	Low
Named by	Leonardo Salgado & Jose Bonaparte
When named	1991
Order	Saurischia (Lizard-hipped)
Type	Sauropodomorpha, Sauropoda

Timeline
Million Years Ago

Late Cretaceous 99-66

Early Cretaceous 144-99

Late Jurassic 159-144

Middle Jurassic 190-159

Early Jurassic 205-190

Late Triassic 227-205

Middle Triassic 242-227

Early Triassic 251-242

Ankylosaurus

Pronounced: *an-kuh-low-SAW-ruhs*

Ankylosaurus was an extremely well-armored dinosaur. Its back and sides were covered with rows of bony spikes, nodules, and plates embedded in the skin. The tail ended in a large bony club, weighing at least 110 pounds (50 kg). The tail club was an excellent weapon, which could be swung to deter any predators. The head was protected by two spikes jutting out from each side. The underbelly was the only vulnerable part of the body, but it could be protected if *Ankylosaurus* crouched down and presented attackers with a body completely covered with bony spikes and plates. *Ankylosaurus*'s size and weight made it slow-moving. Its mouth had a horny, toothless beak for attacking plants, and leaf-shaped cheek teeth for chewing and grinding up food before swallowing. It was one of the very last of the dinosaurs living at the end of the Mesozoic era. The mass extinction then killed all non-avian dinosaurs and many other creatures.

Statistics

Meaning	Fused Lizard
When	Late Cretaceous
Time	71–65 million years ago
Max length	35 feet (10.6 m)
Max height	10 feet (3 m)
Max weight	9,900 pounds (4,500 kg)
Stance	Quadruped
Where	United States (Wyoming, Montana) & Canada (Alberta)
Diet	Herbivore
Activity	Grazing
Intelligence	Low
Named by	Barnum Brown
When named	1908
Order	Ornithischia (Bird-hipped)
Type	Thyreophora, Ankylosauria

Timeline
Million Years Ago

Late Cretaceous
99–66

Early Cretaceous
144–99

Late Jurassic
159–144

Middle Jurassic
190–159

Early Jurassic
205–190

Late Triassic
227–205

Middle Triassic
242–227

Early Triassic
251–242

Kentrosaurus

Pronounced: *kehn-troh-SAW-ruhs*

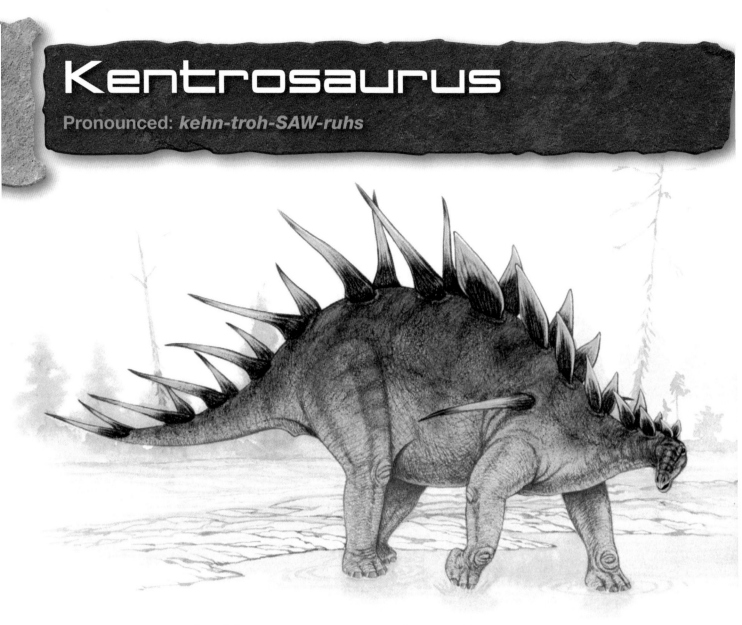

Kentrosaurus is the African cousin of the larger *Stegosaurus*, which is only found in North America. It was an armored dinosaur with a double row of smaller plates over its back from its head. These then became a double row of spikes, up to 24 inches (60 cm) long, from above the hind legs and all along the tail. The spikes and plates were paired rather than staggered, as was the case with *Stegosaurus*, and were embedded in the skin rather than attached to the skeleton. There was an extra spike jutting out from the side of the dinosaur on the shoulder. Its front legs were much shorter than the rear ones, meaning that its head was close to the ground. It fed on low-growing plants such as ferns. It could only move slowly and most likely lived in herds. Its chief predators were the large theropods of the time. Hundreds of bones of *Kentrosaurus* were discovered in 1909 in the Tendaguru Hills of Tanzania, a site rich in fossil finds.

Statistics

Meaning	Spiky Lizard
When	Late Jurassic
Time	154–151 million years ago
Max length	16 feet (5 m)
Max height	8 feet (2.5 m)
Max weight	4,000 pounds (1,800 kg)
Stance	Quadruped
Where	Tanzania
Diet	Herbivore
Activity	Grazing
Intelligence	Low
Named by	Edwin Henning
When named	1915
Order	Ornithischia (Bird-hipped)
Type	Thyreophora, Stegosauria

Timeline
Million Years Ago

Period	Million Years Ago
Late Cretaceous	99–66
Early Cretaceous	144–99
Late Jurassic	159–144
Middle Jurassic	190–159
Early Jurassic	205–190
Late Triassic	227–205
Middle Triassic	242–227
Early Triassic	251–242

An almost complete skeleton of *Ouranosaurus* was discovered in 1966 in the Sahara Desert of Niger, in Africa. Its most distinctive feature is the row of spines that runs down the back, from the neck to almost the end of the tail. These spines are extensions of the individual bones in the backbone and a "sail" of skin most likely covered them. This area of Africa was hot and dry in Early Cretaceous times and a sail would have been useful as a way to regulate temperature. The sail would have been full of blood vessels that could either take in or give off heat, as needed. *Spinosaurus*, a meat-eating dinosaur that also had a sail, lived in the same area at the same time, suggesting that the sails were a response to the climate. *Ouranosaurus* had a tough, horny, toothless beak with a large number of cheek teeth for grinding plants and vegetation.

Statistics

Meaning	Brave Lizard
When	Early Cretaceous
Time	121–112 million years ago
Max length	23 feet (7 m)
Max height	10 feet (3 m)
Max weight	8, 370 pounds (3,800 kg)
Stance	Mainly quadruped
Where	Niger
Diet	Herbivore
Activity	Grazing
Intelligence	Medium
Named by	Philippe Taquet
When named	1976
Order	Ornithischia (Bird-hipped)
Type	Ornithopoda

Timeline
Million Years Ago

Late Cretaceous
99-66

Early Cretaceous
144-99

Late Jurassic
159-144

Middle Jurassic
190-159

Early Jurassic
205-190

Late Triassic
227-205

Middle Triassic
242-227

Early Triassic
251-242

Pachycephalosaurus was one of the last dinosaurs living at the end of the Cretaceous period, alongside *Triceratops* and *Tyrannosaurus rex*, just before the great extinction that wiped out many dinosaurs. The bony lump on its head, which gives *Pachycephalosaurus* its name, was anywhere between about 8 and 10 inches (20 and 25 cm) thick, and was surrounded by small bony spikes and nodules. It was used for headbutting in defense or during fights for power between two *Pachycephalosaurus*, just as male deer do today. The bony spikes and nodules would also have been useful in deterring predators. Skulls of *Pachycephalosaurus* have been found with two types of teeth. In the front part of the jaw, they had the triangular, blade-like teeth associated with a theropod dinosaur. At the back of the jaw, they had leaf-shaped teeth for eating plants. This shows that *Pachycephalosaurus* was an omnivore for at least part of its life, having a mixed diet that included small mammals, and possibly dinosaurs, as well as plants of the Late Cretaceous.

Statistics

Meaning	Thick-headed Lizard
When	Late Cretaceous
Time	71–65 million years ago
Max length	16 feet (5 m)
Max height	8 feet (2.4 m)
Max weight	4,000 pounds (1,800 kg)
Stance	Biped
Where	United States (Montana, Wyoming, Colorado, South Dakota)
Diet	Herbivore
Activity	Grazing
Intelligence	Medium
Named by	Barnum Brown & Erich Schlaiker
When named	1943
Order	Ornithischia (Bird-hipped)
Type	Marginocephalia, Pachycephalosauria

Timeline
Million Years Ago

Late Cretaceous
99-66

Early Cretaceous
144-99

Late Jurassic
159-144

Middle Jurassic
190-159

Early Jurassic
205-190

Late Triassic
227-205

Middle Triassic
242-227

Early Triassic
251-242

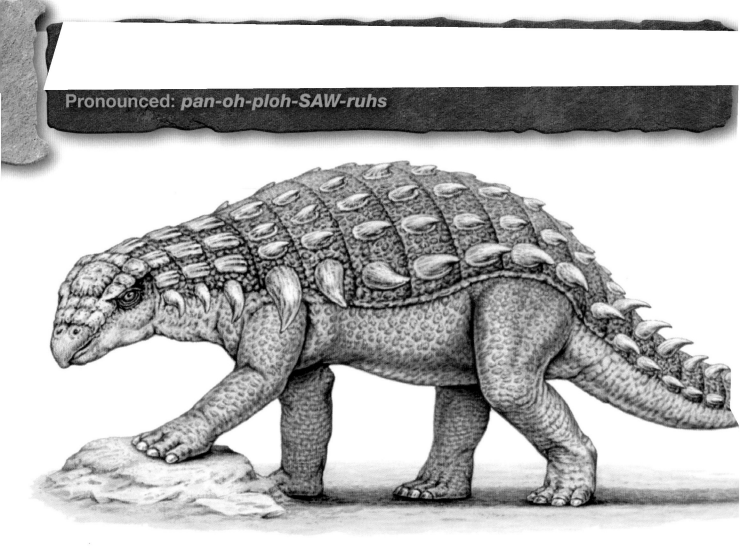

The first fossil remains of *Panoplosaurus* were found in the Judith River Formation in Alberta, Canada. *Panoplosaurus* was the last of the nodosaur group of armored dinosaurs. These were similar to ankylosaurs but did not have a tail club. This dinosaur was heavily armored, with thick, bony, square plates, each with a central ridge, covering the back and embedded in the skin. Both sides were protected by a row of short spikes running from the neck to the end of the tail. The plates covering the head were actually fused to the skull, giving excellent protection. The skull was wide, with a narrow snout which it used to forage along the ground for suitable plants to eat. The front of the mouth was toothless but the cheeks held leaf-shaped teeth for chewing plants. Like ankylosaurs, *Panoplosaurus* would have been prone to overheating. However, long, coiled nasal passages helped to cool the air and blood and to control its brain temperature. Despite its large size, *Panoplosaurus* could have charged at any attacking carnivorous dinosaur to protect itself.

Statistics

Meaning	Fully Armored Lizard
When	Late Cretaceous
Time	84–71 million years ago
Max length	23 feet (7 m)
Max height	7.5 feet (2.3 m)
Max weight	6,600 pounds (3,000 kg)
Stance	Quadruped
Where	United States (Montana, South Dakota, Texas) & Canada (Alberta)
Diet	Herbivore
Activity	Grazing
Intelligence	Low
Named by	Lawrence Lambe
When named	1919
Order	Ornithischia (Bird-hipped)
Type	Thyreophora, Ankylosauria

Timeline
Million Years Ago

Late Cretaceous	99-66
Early Cretaceous	144-99
Late Jurassic	159-144
Middle Jurassic	190-159
Early Jurassic	205-190
Late Triassic	227-205
Middle Triassic	242-227
Early Triassic	251-242

Protoceratops

Pronounced: *proh-toh-SEH-ruh-tahps*

Many hundreds of skeletons of *Protoceratops* have been found, particularly by the expeditions of the American Museum of Natural History to Mongolia, between 1922 and 1925. Numerous eggs and over 100 skeletons were discovered at the Flaming Cliffs, named after the bright red sand, in southern Mongolia. The eggs are torpedo shaped, almost 8 inches (20 cm) long, and were arranged in a spiral pattern in nests. A famous fossil was discovered in 1971 of the skeletons of *Protoceratops* and *Velociraptor* locked in battle. Both fought to the death, until overcome by a sandstorm. *Protoceratops* could really hurt an attacker with its strong beak. It was a common dinosaur during the Late Cretaceous period, living in large herds. It had a bony frill to protect the head and neck, but it did not have any horns. There was a difference between males and females—males were more powerful, had a larger frill, and had a larger bump on the end of the snout. This may have been used for headbutting contests.

Statistics

Meaning	First Horned Face
When	Late Cretaceous
Time	86–71 million years ago
Max length	8 feet (2.5 m)
Max height	3 feet (1 m)
Max weight	880 pounds (400 kg)
Stance	Quadruped
Where	Mongolia & China
Diet	Herbivore
Activity	Grazing
Intelligence	Low
Named by	Walter Granger & William Gregory
When named	1923
Order	Ornithischia (Bird-hipped)
Type	Marginocephalia, Ceratopsia

Timeline
Million Years Ago

Late Cretaceous
99–66

Early Cretaceous
144–99

Late Jurassic
159–144

Middle Jurassic
190–159

Early Jurassic
205–190

Late Triassic
227–205

Middle Triassic
242–227

Early Triassic
251–242

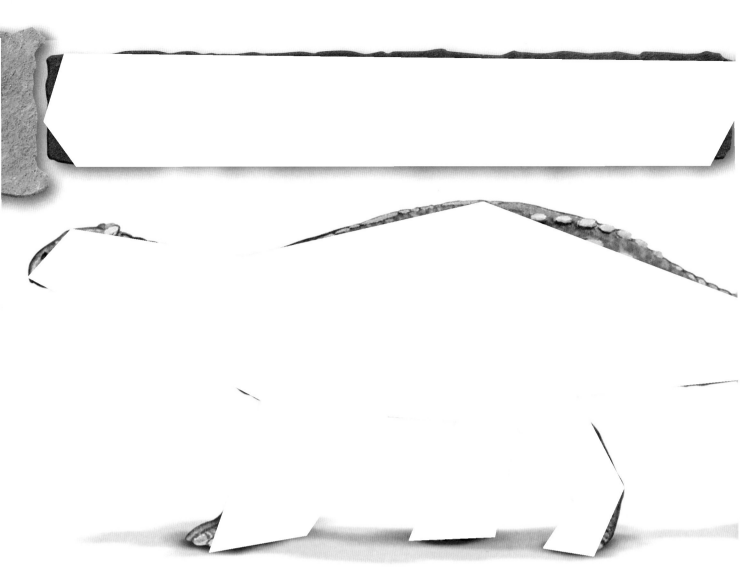

Scelidosaurus has only been found in marine deposits in Dorset, England, that are more commonly known for ichthyosaur and plesiosaur remains. The carcasses of *Scelidosaurus* were probably washed down a river into the sea to become fossilized. It is a fairly primitive dinosaur, considered to be an early ankylosaur. The whole of the upper side of the body was covered by parallel rows of bony scutes (horny or bony plates) and a row of short spines to give protection from predators. The small, horny beak had sharp edges and leaf-shaped cheek teeth for eating plants. The rear legs were longer and more powerful than the front ones, but it was still a dinosaur that walked on all four legs. The first bones named as *Scelidosaurus* were much later found to be a mix from several kinds of dinosaurs. A dinosaur skeleton found in 1863 was then given the name *Scelidosaurus*.

Statistics

Meaning	Rear Leg Lizard
When	Early Jurassic
Time	202–190 million years ago
Max length	13 feet (4 m)
Max height	3.6 feet (1.1 m)
Max weight	770 pounds (350 kg)
Stance	Quadruped
Where	England & United States (Arizona)
Diet	Herbivore
Activity	Grazing
Intelligence	Low
Named by	Richard Owen
When named	1863
Order	Ornithischia (Bird-hipped)
Type	Thyreophora, Ankylosauria

Timeline
Million Years Ago

Late Cretaceous
99–66

Early Cretaceous
144–99

Late Jurassic
159–144

Middle Jurassic
190–159

Early Jurassic
205–190

Late Triassic
227–205

Middle Triassic
242–227

Early Triassic
251–242

This armored dinosaur was distinguished by two rows of alternating bony plates, over 24 inches (60 cm) high, along the back and tail. The plates contained blood vessels and most likely acted as temperature regulators, either taking in or giving off heat. They may also have been used for display. *Stegosaurus* had spikes, up to 3.2 feet (1 m) long, on the end of its flexible tail, which it used to defend itself. There were either four or eight spikes depending on the species. Bony scutes or studs protected parts of the body. The small head was held very close to the ground, as the front legs were much shorter than the rear ones. This was because *Stegosaurus* was descended from earlier two-legged dinosaurs. Its beak was toothless, but there were cheek teeth behind it. *Stegosaurus* had a strong bite, similar to that of a cow today, and fed off low vegetation, or plants, such as ferns and cycads. *Stegosaurus* is famous for its tiny brain, only the size of a walnut, making it one of the least intelligent dinosaurs.

Statistics

Meaning	Roofed Lizard
When	Late Jurassic
Time	156–144 million years ago
Max length	30 feet (9 m)
Max height	9 feet (2.75 m) at hips
Max weight	6,000 pounds (2,700 kg)
Stance	Quadruped
Where	United States (Wyoming, Colorado, Utah, Oklahoma)
Diet	Herbivore
Activity	Browsing, possibly in herds
Intelligence	Low
Named by	Othniel Charles Marsh
When named	1877
Order	Ornithischia (Bird-hipped)
Type	Thyreophora, Stegosauria

Timeline
Million Years Ago

Late Cretaceous
99–66

Early Cretaceous
144–99

Late Jurassic
159–144

Middle Jurassic
190–159

Early Jurassic
205–190

Late Triassic
227–205

Middle Triassic
242–227

Early Triassic
251–242

Therizinosaurus was a rather strange-looking, very tall dinosaur with a feathered body and longer feathers on its arms. It was discovered in 1948 and has puzzled scientists since then. At first, it was thought that it was a turtle-like lizard. It takes its name from three long, curving claws on each hand. The longest of these was 36 inches (91 cm) long. Their purpose has been much disputed, but it's likely that they were used for gathering branches and fronds of plants. The long claws would also have acted as good weapons in deterring predators. This was necessary, as *Therizinosaurus* was slow-moving. *Therizinosaurus* may have squatted down and fed in a similar way to a gorilla. It had a weak neck, a small head, and a toothless beak. It was an extremely unusual theropod with small, leaf-shaped teeth, pointing to a herbivorous diet, although it probably ate small animals.

Statistics

Meaning	Scythe Lizard
When	Late Cretaceous
Time	84–71 million years ago
Max length	36 feet (11 m)
Max height	13 feet (4 m)
Max weight	6,600 pounds (3,000 kg)
Stance	Biped
Where	Mongolia
Diet	Probably herbivore
Activity	Probably grazing
Intelligence	Medium
Named by	Evgenii Maleev
When named	1954
Order	Saurischia (Lizard-hipped)
Type	Theropoda, Tetanurae, Segnosauria

Timeline
Million Years Ago

Late Cretaceous
99-66

Early Cretaceous
144-99

Late Jurassic
159-144

Middle Jurassic
190-159

Early Jurassic
205-190

Late Triassic
227-205

Middle Triassic
242-227

Early Triassic
251-242

Triceratops is named after the three horns that protrude from the large bony frill that covered the head and protected the neck. The front horn on the snout was short, while the horns over each eye were up to 5 feet (1.5 m) long, with sharp tips. *Triceratops* would have probably charged any predator, using a combination of its weight and its horns and frill to fight off any potential attack. One of these predators was *Tyrannosaurus rex*, whose bite marks have been found in bones belonging to *Triceratops*. Around the edge of the frill were small, bony spikes for added protection. The skull was enormous, forming almost one-third of the entire length of the dinosaur. Many skulls and horns show scars from damage during combat. *Triceratops* may have locked horns in fights with other *Triceratops*. It was a common dinosaur, living at the end of the dinosaur era. It lived in herds, feeding off low-growing plants such as cycads and ferns.

Statistics

Meaning	Three-horned Face
When	Late Cretaceous
Time	71–65 million years ago
Max length	30 feet (9 m)
Max height	10 feet (3 m) at hips
Max weight	22,000 pounds (10,000 kg)
Stance	Quadruped
Where	United States (Colorado, Montana, Wyoming, South Dakota) & Canada (Alberta, Saskatchewan)
Diet	Herbivore
Activity	Grazing in herds
Intelligence	Medium
Named by	Othniel Charles Marsh
When named	1889
Order	Ornithischia (Bird-hipped)
Type	Marginocephalia, Ceratopsia

Timeline
Million Years Ago

Period	Million Years Ago
Late Cretaceous	99–66
Early Cretaceous	144–99
Late Jurassic	159–144
Middle Jurassic	190–159
Early Jurassic	205–190
Late Triassic	227–205
Middle Triassic	242–227
Early Triassic	251–242

Just One

Amargasaurus is one of the best-known sauropods of its time period, even though only one skeleton of this dinosaur has been found. The skeleton, unearthed in Argentina in 1984, is almost complete and includes most of the skull. This fossil find led to the naming of the dinosaur in 1991.

GLOSSARY

avian: having to do with birds

carnivorous: having to do with a carnivore, or an animal that eats meat

cheek teeth: teeth that have a rounded surface for grinding up food

deter: to stop something from happening

fossil: the remains or traces of plants and animals from the past

gastrolith: a stone eaten by an animal to help grind up food in the digestive system

herbivorous: having to do with a herbivore, or an animal that eats plants

omnivore: an animal that eats both meat and plants

regulate: to set or adjust to the amount of something, such as heat

sauropod: a group of dinosaurs from the Jurassic and Cretaceous that walked on all fours, had a long neck and tail, and a small head

theropod: a group of carnivorous dinosaurs that walked on two feet

FOR MORE INFORMATION

Books

Dixon, Dougal. *Jurassic Dinosaurs*. Mission Viejo, CA: Quarto Library, 2020.

Kelly, Erin Suzanne. *Dinosaurs*. New York, NY: Children's Press, an imprint of Scholastic Inc., 2021.

Magrin, Frederica, and Denise Muir. *The Great Book of Dinosaurs*. New York, NY: Sterling Children's Books, 2020.

Websites

Ankylosaurus Facts for Kids
www.dkfindout.com/us/dinosaurs-and-prehistoric-life/dinosaurs/ankylosaurus/
See a diagram and read more facts about this dinosaur, among others.

Meet Some Deadly Dinos!
www.natgeokids.com/uk/discover/animals/prehistoric-animals/meet-some-deadly-dinos/
Find out more about even more awesome dinosaurs.

Publisher's note to parents and teachers: Our editors have reviewed the websites listed here to make sure they're suitable for students. However, websites may change frequently. Please note that students should always be supervised when they access the internet.

INDEX